Original title:
The Islands' Heartbeat

Copyright © 2025 Creative Arts Management OÜ
All rights reserved.

Author: Jude Lancaster
ISBN HARDBACK: 978-1-80581-667-6
ISBN PAPERBACK: 978-1-80581-194-7
ISBN EBOOK: 978-1-80581-667-6

Heartstrings of Sunlit Sands

On sandy shores where crabs do dance,
A flip-flop's flight becomes romance.
Seagulls caw with silly flair,
As beach balls bounce without a care.

Sunbathers roast like crispy fries,
While sunscreen glistens on their thighs.
Kids chase waves with giggles bright,
And sandcastles tremble in delight.

Dance of the Glistening Waves

Waves waltz in with a playful push,
Shells twirl around like a blushing bush.
Surfboards tumble, a clumsy sight,
As dolphins giggle in the twilight.

Flippered friends flip high and low,
Doing the limbo with quite a show.
Mermaids laugh, their hair a mess,
All just part of the ocean's jest.

Song of the Forgotten Harbors

Old boats creak like aging men,
Whispering tales that never end.
Fish in barrels sing off-key,
While seagulls join in harmony.

Rusty anchors tap their feet,
To the rhythm of the tide's heartbeat.
Crabs tell jokes beneath the pier,
Creating laughter that we all hear.

The Deep's Gentle Thrum

Beneath the waves, the fish hold court,
With jellyfish making a fine report.
Octopuses juggle seaweed fast,
While clownfish giggle, having a blast.

Starfish lay in a fancy pose,
Winking at turtles, striking a rose.
The sea's a circus beneath the foam,
Where every creature feels at home.

Songs of the Wanderer's Isle

On shores where coconuts dance with a grin,
A parrot sings jokes in the warm ocean wind.
Laughter erupts like the waves on the sand,
As seashells cheer, forming a quirky band.

Turtles wear shades, strutting in style,
While crabs do the cha-cha, it's all worthwhile.
Under the sun, with a coconut drink,
The seaweed waltzes, who needs to think?

Flickers in the Crystal Blue

Beneath the waves, the fish throw a rave,
With disco balls made from shells, how brave!
Dolphins are DJs, spinning tunes with flair,
While sea cucumbers float without a care.

Starfish dance like they've lost their way,
Doing the twist on a fine coral bay.
"Catch me if you can!" the jellyfish tease,
As they float away with effortless ease.

Essence of Salt and Sun

A crab with a top hat leads the parade,
While flamingos gossip, unafraid.
In the sun's embrace, they share a good laugh,
As seagulls critique the crab's silly gaff.

Wave after wave of salty delight,
Makes even the fish feel a bit polite.
But beware of the seagulls, they steal your fries,
With a swoop and a dive, they're oh-so-sly!

Dreamweaver of the Mystic Shores

On the beach, a sandcastle dreams of being grand,
As seagulls plot to create a new band.
Mermaids giggle, weaving garlands of sea,
While fish practice ballet, it's quite a spree.

With every splash, a new tale unfolds,
Of turtles that dance and stories that's told.
A starfish with swagger claims the spotlight,
In the heart of the ocean, life is just right.

Currents of an Untamed Heart

In the shallow cove, fish dance and play,
Jellyfish waltz in a whimsical fray.
Sea cucumbers snooze, all quiet and neat,
While crabs do the cha-cha on their tiny feet.

The waves giggle softly with each little push,
Making sandcastles melt with a gentle whoosh.
Turtles wear shades while catching some rays,
As seagulls gossip in their feathered ways.

Rhythmic Whispers of the Trade Winds

Breezes whoosh by like a barrel of laughs,
Umbrellas dance freely in silly drafts.
Coconut palms sway, waving their hands,
Winking at tourists who miss all their plans.

Kites drift skyward, caught in a swirl,
As children chase dreams with a joyful twirl.
Mermaids applaud from the depths of the sea,
While sailors sing shanties, slightly off-key.

Dreams Anchored in Sapphire Waters

On the beach, dreams float in bright-colored sails,
While flip-flops gossip and swap childhood tales.
A pelican dives for lunch with a flair,
Cracking jokes with a splash, without a care.

The sun plays peek-a-boo through clouds of delight,
As waves tell stories under the moonlight.
Crabbing becomes a wild, giggly race,
As everyone runs, with sand on their face!

Heartbeat of the Shoreline Shadows

Sand dollars hide, pretending to be shy,
While starfish throw parties as they float by.
The tide comes and goes, like a fickle friend,
Chasing seagulls around the shoreline bend.

With hearts full of laughter, we dance on the sand,
Making memories, right hand in hand.
Under the sun, we craft tales full of cheer,
As the waves hum a tune we all want to hear.

Whispers of the Tidal Winds

A seagull stole my sandwich,
It's a bold culinary thief!
The waves chuckled softly,
As I searched for my lost beef.

The salty breeze is laughing,
It tickles my nose with glee.
Even the fish are snickering,
At my failed attempts to flee.

The crabs dance in the sand,
With moves that make me grin.
They challenge me to a duel,
But I just want to swim!

Oh listen to the water's song,
It's full of splashes and splatters.
It's a concert of playful tides,
Where laughter truly matters.

Pulse of the Forgotten Shores

Once I tripped on a seashell,
It sent me flying like a kite.
The ocean roared with laughter,
As I landed in a fright.

The sand shrugged with amusement,
While beach balls rolled nearby.
Seagulls perched on their throne,
Watching me and starting to cry.

A turtle nodded wisely,
As I flailed and tried to stand.
He said, 'Just relax and breathe,'
While I danced in the soft sand.

The sun winked from its perch,
Casting rays like playful darts.
Each wave a chuckle shared,
Reminding me of joyful hearts.

Echoes Beneath Palm Fronds

Beneath the palms I found a treasure,
A flip-flop freed by the tide.
But who could wear just one shoe,
In this sun-kissed, reckless ride?

The coconuts are gossiping,
'Check out that tourist, so lost!'
While I chase rare beach critters,
Wondering what's really the cost.

A crab scuttled with swagger,
Each step a sassy display.
But I laughed and waved my arms,
As he swiftly loomed away.

The breeze carried all my giggles,
As I danced like a silly fool.
In the shades of those palm fronds,
Life's silliness is the golden rule.

Rhythms of the Coral Coves

Down at the cove, I found my groove,
Surrounded by fish doing the twist.
They called me over, 'Join the dance!'
A party I couldn't resist!

With flippers flapping and tails a-swish,
Even the octopuses joined in,
Painting marvelous strokes of joy,
Each move was a splash, pure sin.

The seaweed waved like it was grooving,
To the beats of the playful sea.
In this underwater rave of colors,
I found my inner jellyfish glee.

As the sun began to dip, and sparkle,
We bid adieu to the day.
But the laughter floated and lingered,
In these coral coves, come what may.

Threads of Time Within a Shell

In a shell, time's a tricky prank,
Tick-tock whispers of a fishy tank.
Seagulls gossip like old school friends,
While a crab waves his claw, it never ends.

A flip-flop lands on a sandy throne,
Dancing to beats of a calypso tone.
Hermit crabs strut in their borrowed homes,
Debating the merits of sea foam poems.

The sun sets with a cheerful grin,
As beach chairs fight the day's last din.
A coconut falls, the crowd will cheer,
This is the best soap opera of the year.

Tides bring laughter, waves bring cheer,
Shells tell stories we long to hear.
With each tide, a new tale to tell,
In the hollow echoes of a shell.

The Aroma of the Endless Sea

Breezes carry scents from a taco stand,
Mixing together in a twisty strand.
Fish fry dances with salty air,
While dolphins laugh with a knowing stare.

Driftwood humor sticks to the sand,
As starfish plot a vacation, oh so grand.
Lobsters in sunglasses strut down the beach,
Waving at tourists, within arm's reach.

Seagulls squawk about lost treasures,
Trading stories for sunbathing pleasures.
Pineapple hats and tan lines galore,
Who knew the ocean had a comic store?

As night descends, laughter takes flight,
Party lights flicker, a dazzling sight.
With krill on the menu and fun so free,
The aroma of joy wafts over the sea.

Traces of the Moonlit Pacific

Under moonlight, waves wear a smile,
Fish throw parties; it's quite a while.
Turtles in tutus glide by with flair,
While jellyfish twirl in a wobbly pair.

A chorus of crickets sings by the shore,
While octopuses play cards and roar.
Sandcastles tattle on the tides they know,
Telling tales of beach balls in tow.

The stars are bright, they blink and tease,
Barbeque smoke drifts on a gentle breeze.
A crab in a top hat gives a sly wink,
While mermaids debate the best drink to drink.

With laughter rising like the moon's soft glow,
The ocean's vibes are a funny show.
No hint of trouble, only gleeful cheer,
In the heart of the Pacific, nothing's austere.

Chronicles of the Wind-Swept Isle

Windswept whispers, secrets spill,
As coconuts fall with a gentle thrill.
Flip-flops chatter on cobblestone,
Creating tales of their own, unknown.

The toucans wear hats, they dance with grace,
As parakeets join in the lively chase.
Lizards in shades discuss local lore,
While sea turtles pretend to be hardcore.

Sunsets are painted in laughter's hue,
As beachcombers hunt for treasures new.
A crab plays guitar, its shell polished bright,
Encouraging sandcastles to party all night.

Chronicles burst from the waves and air,
As the island sways in a festive affair.
With each gust of wind, a giggle or two,
The isle's heart beats, and we all feel brand new.

Harmony of the Sunlit Sands

Waves giggle at the shore,
Sand tickles your toes,
Seagulls dive for popcorn,
What a show, heaven knows!

Crabs in tuxedos scurry,
Shellfish gossip with flair,
The sun winks and chuckles,
As we bask without care.

Children build castles tall,
While parents sip their drinks,
A sandman crumbles and falls,
Oops! Now he hardly blinks.

Breeze whispers in laughter,
Jellyfish juggle in blue,
Laughter rolls like the tides,
What a splendid view!

Dance of the Pelagic Spirits

Fish wear hats and dance,
Mermaids giggle and swoon,
Seashells tap their tiny feet,
While the starfish croon.

Whales tell jokes in deep blues,
Dolphins jump with some grace,
The ocean's rhythm is wild,
What a funny place!

A crab plays a tuba,
Octopus holds a mic,
The seaweed sways wildly,
As jellyfish ride their bike.

Currents swirl in delight,
Anemones shake with glee,
Every splash is a giggle,
Underwater jamboree!

Lullaby of Palm Fronds

Palm fronds sway to a tune,
Whispers of the balmy air,
Coconuts drop like bad puns,
Hitting folks unaware.

Leaves gossip in the breeze,
With stories of sunbeam fights,
Grasshoppers hop like crazy,
While the fireflies, oh, they light!

Lizards lounge without shame,
Basking in the sunshine's glow,
Tiny parrots crack up loudly,
Like they stole the whole show.

As twilight brings a hush,
Stars peek out, twinkling bright,
The palms whisper sweet nothings,
In this island's soft night.

Cadence of the Eternal Horizon

The sun paints laughs in gold,
Clouds puff up with pride,
While waves keep a rhythm,
Oh, the sea's joyful ride!

Kites canoodles in the air,
Birds tweet about their dreams,
The horizon spreads like butter,
On toast with sunny beams.

Breezes stomp through the trees,
They dance like clumsy folks,
While shadows sprout mischievous,
Playing funny little jokes.

Finally, the day takes a bow,
As stars come out to play,
The night sings with a grin,
In this endless ballet!

Hymn of the Seafoam Symphony

A crab with a hat plays the fiddle,
While dolphins dance, not a little.
Splashing water in rhythm bright,
As fish join the chorus of delight.

Seagulls squawk in a silly way,
Belly flops from a seal at play.
The sun winks down with a grin,
While waves tickle toes with a spin.

Octopus holds a conga line,
With starfish cheering, feeling fine.
The beach ball rolls, the tide takes it,
Creating giggles, can't resist it.

So raise your glass of seaweed juice,
For the ocean's tunes, let's cut loose!
Each wave brings laughter, splashes loud,
In a symphony, we are proud.

Lullabies of the Ocean's Embrace

Shhh, the moon tells tales to the tide,
As sleepy waves in the sand abide.
Crabs dance under silvery beams,
While seaweed hums in soothing dreams.

Starfish on pillows, cozy and bright,
Whisper secrets of the night.
Seashells giggle, echo their glee,
As the ocean sighs, 'Come dream with me!'

Jellyfish float, their dance a glow,
While clownfish tease in a playful show.
The night sky twinkles, stars lend sight,
For the ocean cradles you tight.

With every lull, the waves do sigh,
As breezy whispers kite high in the sky.
The ocean rocks you, soft as a feather,
In this funny world, we drift together.

The Breath of Remote Horizons

Beyond the waves, there's a laughing breeze,
Carrying stories through dancing trees.
An island's grin, so wide and bright,
While coconuts chuckle, taking flight.

Pelicans gossip, wearing shades,
On piers built high with wobbly braids.
A turtle rolls, wants to take a turn,
While silly fish wait for their learned.

The sky blushes pink with a wink,
As sailors ponder what they think.
With every wave, the laughter spreads,
From jellyfish kids to anchovy heads.

So toast to the winds that sway and spin,
In waters where giggles do begin.
With every splash and every tear,
There's fun and joy; let's give a cheer!

Nautical Dreams Along the Coast

In boats made of laughter and sticky goo,
Sailors dream dreams with a colorful crew.
A parrot squawks while taking the stage,
Whispering jokes from a nautical page.

Waves play peekaboo with the sun,
As fish take turns in a water gun.
The clouds join in, with cotton candy,
Creating giggles, oh-so-handy!

A lighthouse twirls in the morning light,
With a wink and a dance, what a sight!
Shells start singing in harmony soon,
While starfish tap to the ocean's tune.

In this whimsical world, let's all play,
And tickle the dolphins in a funny way.
So cast your lines, set your hearts free,
For nautical dreams are the best—yippee!

Currents of Untamed Freedom

Drifting on waves with a grin,
Fishy tales in the air spin.
Seagulls swoop and steal my fries,
Winking at me, oh how time flies!

Crabs wear shells like tuxedos neat,
Shuffling sideways with grooving feet.
The sun's a spotlight on this stage,
While jellyfish dance with such rage!

Laughter bubbles, currents swirl,
A seaweed wig adds a twist and twirl.
In this water's wild embrace,
I find my wiggles and my place!

Unruly tides toss me around,
In this aquatic circus, I'm spellbound.
Splashes echo my joyful shout,
Freedom calls, there's never doubt!

Heartstrings of the Blue Abyss

Bubbles rise like giggles in glee,
Squid chase mermaids, what a sight to see!
Octopuses play the ukulele tunes,
As dolphins join in, under the moons.

Crappy puns from clownfish friends,
Making waves where laughter never ends.
Treasure chests filled with socks,
Splashing about on the ocean rocks!

Seashells whisper in silly frost,
Waving goodbye to the socks we've lost.
Beneath the surface, friendships twine,
Through coral colors, all divine!

Giggling sea sponges join the parade,
As anemones sway in masquerade.
Life's a party in this azure dream,
With heartstrings pulsing in a gleam!

Breath of the Coastal Flora

Palm trees sway with a teasing laugh,
Whispering jokes as they catch the draft.
Coconuts drop with a plop and a thud,
While sandcastles crumble in giggling mud!

Breezes ruffle my beachy hat,
I chase seagulls, how about that?
The sun's warmth tickles my sandy toes,
As I dance with crabs, in funny shows!

Come join the party where flowers bloom,
With petals twirling, dispelling gloom.
Even the tide changes its pace,
Breaking out in a funny embrace!

Colors swirl from dusk till dawn,
In this coastal wonder, I'm never torn.
With every gust, life's a joyful chant,
I sing along, oh yes I can!

Embrace of the Salted Mist

Mist rolls in with a ticklish tease,
Bringing salty whispers with ocean breeze.
Sand between toes like nature's tickle,
Makes me dance with a hop and a wiggle!

Sea otters sport sparkly berets,
Making ripples in humorous ways.
The lighthouse winks with a feathery light,
As I strut my stuff in seaweed delight!

Nautical nonsense unfolds all around,
With every wave, a funny sound.
The moon is chuckling, casting its glow,
On this nightly stage, we steal the show!

So here's to the rhythms, the fun and the mist,
In a world where laughter can't be dismissed.
Let's ride this wave, with hearts filled with cheer,
For in this salty dance, we find our dear!

Loops of the Endless Wave

Waves giggle as they play,
Chasing crabs that scurry away.
Seagulls squawk in silly glee,
Surfboards dance like bumblebees.

Sandy toes in a hilarious fight,
With flip-flops flying left and right.
Tide pools hold a wiggly prize,
A starfish grins with googly eyes.

Laughter bursts from every shore,
While fishermen drop their bait once more.
The ocean jokes with every swell,
As shells giggle of secrets they tell.

So raise a toast to waves that tease,
And ride the current with greatest ease.
In this quirky, frothy spot,
Where fun's the aim, forget the plot.

Twilight's Kiss on the Solitary Rock

As day fades, the sun gives a wink,
While crickets start to serenade and sync.
A hermit crab dons a fancy hat,
Giving style tips to an unsuspecting cat.

The sky blushes in glorious hues,
While distant waves sing a ballad of blues.
A star comes out wearing a bright bowtie,
As fireflies flash like they're saying hi.

On the rock, a seagull makes a stand,
Practicing moves for a dance-off planned.
But a sudden gust sends him in a whirl,
He lands awkwardly, sending shells to twirl.

So celebrate each twilight with mirth,
Where laughter dances with the earth.
Under stars that twinkle and tease,
Life's a comedy; let's laugh with ease.

Ebbing Dreams and Starlit Paths

The moon whispers as it casts its light,
Following shadows in the dead of night.
A dog barks at a shimmering star,
Thinking it's just a distant, shiny car.

Seashells giggle in the sandy bay,
Arguing about who's best at play.
A jellyfish jives with rhythm and grace,
While clueless fish swim in the wrong place.

Coconuts roll like they're on a spree,
Hiding secrets like coconut-free tea.
Bubbles rise from gurgles below,
As sleepy digs jest in night's soft glow.

So dance with dreams on paths of starlight,
Let laughter be your beacon tonight.
For every wave that genuinely sways,
Sings silly songs of sunlit days.

Legacy of the Ancient Driftwood

There's wisdom in the driftwood's grin,
Tales of seas that made it spin.
A crab cracks jokes at its wooden peers,
While the ocean chuckles, wiping its tears.

The sunken treasure twinkles from the bay,
Winking at waves that come out to play.
An octopus reads from a soggy book,
Pausing for applause that no one took.

Seagulls debate who reigns in the skies,
With triumphant squawks that pierce and rise.
The driftwood nods, proud of its fame,
In tales of joy, it plays a game.

So honor the stories in sandy repose,
And share the laughter that forever grows.
For in every splinter, there lies a delight,
A legacy of humor, shining bright.

Whirl of Crystals and Waves

Seashells whisper secrets, quite absurd,
As fish wear tiny hats, oh how they've stirred.
Sandcastles squabble, their towers too tall,
While crabs practice salsa and dance at the mall.

Flip-flops chatter gossip, just can't keep still,
The sun throws a party on every hill.
Laughter erupts as seagulls conspire,
To steal all the snacks that we dare to acquire.

Waves tickle toes, a giggle ensues,
Swim trunks do the cha-cha, it's all good news.
The ocean hums tune, a whimsical song,
In this playful realm, where we all belong.

So grab your beach towel, join in the fun,
With sunblock aplenty, let's soak in the sun.
For laughter and joy are what we'll achieve,
In waters so shallow, we never want to leave.

In the Shade of Tropical Reveries

Under palm trees swinging, monkeys swing by,
With sunglasses on, they wave from the sky.
Coconuts giggle, as they take a fall,
Rolling down hills, they bounce, and they sprawl.

Hammocks are grinning, swaying with glee,
While pineapples gossip about life's great spree.
Sipping cold drinks with umbrellas so bright,
We toast to the sand, and laugh at the sight.

Flip-flops engaged in a race down the shore,
A victory dance, oh what's in store!
Sandy toes high-five as stars start to shine,
In this goofy paradise, life feels divine.

The sun dips low, as the crickets take stage,
Each night a new story, a humorous page.
In the shade of dreams where the fun never ends,
We gather as one, with our giggling friends.

Resonance of Misty Mornings

Morning mist rolls in, like a blanket of fluff,
While roosters debate who's making the rough.
Dewdrops share tales of their nighttime plight,
As lizards do yoga, feeling quite light.

The coffee pot whistles a melody sweet,
While turtles make breakfast, without missing a beat.
Bananas play poker, all yellow and round,
With laughter and fun, they spread joy around.

Waves yawn and stretch as the sun lights the scene,
While dolphins do flips, oh what a routine!
Parrots on branches gossip in colors,
Pondering their lives, like spirited scholars.

So here's to the mornings that tickle our nose,
With funny surprises wherever one goes.
In the dance of dawn's light where silliness stays,
We kick off our dreams in a sunbeam's embrace.

Shimmering Footprints on Serene Shores

Footprints dash across like a playful parade,
As seagulls take selfies, their laughter displayed.
Sand dollars chuckle, flipping through the day,
While starfish form bands and start to play.

Waves roll in softly, like whispers of glee,
Shells gather around for the grand jubilee.
Sandworm attempts to wiggle and dance,
Inviting the crabs for a chance romance.

As sunset arrives, paints the skies pink,
Kites dive and swoop, putting on a wink.
Breezes are giggling, tickling our cheeks,
In a world where the joy is found in the peaks.

So join all the antics, the silliness here,
In shimmering footprints, let's spread the cheer.
For life's but a canvas, splashed with delight,
Under vibrant horizons, where everything's bright.

Soul of the Seabreeze

A seagull once wore a funny hat,
It danced on the wind, imagine that!
With flip-flops on, it strutted about,
Singing tunes, oh, what a clout!

The breeze tickled trees, made them laugh,
While crabs joined in, a comical staff.
They juggled shells like they were pro,
Just a day in the sun, stealing the show!

Pelicans played cards at the pier,
Betting with fish, oh dear, oh dear!
A dolphin cheered with a fishy grin,
Who knew that good times could lead to a win?

As the sun dipped low in peachy delight,
The seabreeze whispered, "What a sight!"
Laughter echoed, joy found its way,
In this jolly world, let's dance and play!

Murmurs of the Hidden Coves

In hidden coves where secrets spill,
The crabs tell jokes with snappy thrill.
A turtle hands out shells for laughs,
While seaweed sways like quirky halves.

"Why did the fish swim on a board?"
"To catch the waves, and not get bored!"
The chatter swirled in salty air,
As otters rolled without a care.

At sunset's touch, the gossip soared,
A dolphin winked as he scored.
They splashed around, in playful dives,
Sharing giggles of aquatic lives.

Coves held laughter, bright with mirth,
In harmony with the ocean's girth.
Each ripple carried a joyful tune,
Under the watchful eye of the moon!

Tides of Time and Memory

The tide tickled toes with every wave,
As memories danced, bold and brave.
"Remember when a clam wore a bow?"
It pranced about, a star of the show!

Time swayed like sea grass in delight,
With fish gossiping, what a sight!
Each splash was a chuckle, each foam a grin,
Reminiscing tales where laughter begins.

Seashells whispered stories of old,
Of pirate jokes and treasures untold.
A shrimp with a flair for the dramatic,
Left all in stitches, oh, what a comic!

With each ebb, the memories glowed,
As sunset's colors humor bestowed.
The tides carried laughter, echoing wide,
In this ocean of joy where we all abide!

Song of the Sheltered Bay

In a sheltered bay where giggles bloom,
The wind plays tunes in a sunny room.
A crab composed a symphony grand,
With a rusty fork as his baton in hand!

The oysters clashed in their pearl-clad suits,
While dolphins donned their flashy boots.
"Let's start a band!" a starfish declared,
With improvised beats, earthiness paired.

Seashells chirped in a chorus divine,
Harmonizing sweet with the mariner's wine.
Tales of adventure, laughter, and fun,
In this sheltered bay, worries are done.

As moonlight cascaded, the music soared,
With each frothy wave, new joy was poured.
A melody bright, a chorus of cheer,
In this bay of laughter, we hold so dear!

Tangle of Sea and Sky

On a lazy afternoon, birds flew wild,
They dodged the sun, like a playful child.
A fish jumped high, a splash went wide,
While on the shore, a crab tried to hide.

The waves whispered jokes to the beach so fine,
As seashells giggled under the sunshine.
A dolphin danced, wearing shades of blue,
While seaweed swayed, like it knew what to do.

Tides waltzed around, like it was a ball,
And sea urchins grinned, feeling ten feet tall.
The sky blushed pink, with clouds in a twist,
As oceanic friends parted with a tryst.

So here we lay, in a quirky sea dream,
Where laughter bubbles, and nothing's as it seems.
The sun sets low, casting shadows so spry,
As waves serenade, under the broad sky.

Chords of the Twilight Tide

As daylight melts into a purple swirl,
Jellyfish jive, with a twirl and a whirl.
Starfish strum ukuleles on coral beds,
While crabs tap dance, on their little red heads.

The moon hangs low, a cheeky old bulb,
Fish flash smiles; they're in on the schmooze.
An octopus, wise, plays chess with a seal,
While echoing laughter, from the night, feels real.

Mermaids gossip, in giggles and sighs,
About the lost pirate with swashbuckling eyes.
The seaweed stirs, as if part of the show,
When wind plays the tune, and the tide starts to flow.

The night hums softly, with rhythms so bright,
As oceanic creatures dance into the night.
To every wave crashing, all share the refrain,
A melody spun from the sea and the grain.

Out of the Depths, I Rise

A clam told a turtle, "I'm feeling quite bold,"
"Me too," said the turtle, "I'll wear your gold!"
They hatched a plan, to find treasure so dear,
In a sunken ship, filled with laughter and cheer.

A seahorse dressed up, for a party so grand,
With beads made of bubbles, to suit every hand.
Octopus barista served coffee in shells,
While sea stars performed with their twinkling spells.

They broke into song, with a chorus so nice,
While fish in tuxedos danced once or twice.
The waters around them twinkled with glee,
As they sang of adventures beneath the blue sea.

But then came a wave, with a twist and a flip,
And sent our dear friends on a watery trip.
With laughter and splashes, they rose to the sky,
In a frolicsome splash, where dependencies fly!

Tales Carried by the Zephyr

Once upon a breeze, a tale took its flight,
Of a seagull named Bert, who fancied the night.
He charmed all the waves with his croaky old song,
And danced with the wind, where the gulls all belong.

The clouds joined in, with a fluffy soft grin,
As dolphins high-fived with a flip of their fin.
The zephyr whispered secrets, to each rock and shell,
While a clam plotted schemes, to create a grand spell.

But soon came a storm, dropping galleon dreams,
Where fish donned their raincoats, or so it all seems.
They splashed through the puddles, shared jokes so absurd,
While crabs in the currents listened, quite stirred.

And when calm returned, the laughter was sweet,
With stories of mishaps, and dancers on feet.
So here on the shore, with a grin wide and bright,
The tales of the zephyr wear sunlight like light.

Voices carried on the Wind

Seagulls squawk in playful jest,
Waves tickle toes, the sun's a guest.
A crab wears shades like a beach king,
Laughter echoes, the ocean sings.

Flip-flops squeak on sandy shores,
Shells debate what fun is in stores.
Turtles skate in sunlit glee,
While fish swap tales of the deep sea.

Kites swirl high on breezy threads,
Kids chase dreams where the ocean spreads.
Cocktails dance with tiny umbrellas,
While the sun naps, we're all just fella's.

The breeze teases, giggles take flight,
As dusk wraps all in gentle night.
Stars wink down, the moon's a pal,
Together we, in joy, we shall.

Silken Threads of Sand and Sky

Sandcastles rise with a royal grace,
Portly crabs march at a plucky pace.
Seashells gossip about their plight,
While sandy dogs race in pure delight.

Clouds wear hats made of cotton candy,
While fishermen sing tunes so dandy.
Waves shout back with splashes of cheer,
As beach balls bounce, the fun is near.

Sunsets wear pajamas of orange and red,
Stars play hide and seek, in dreamlike bed.
The horizon winks at a passing kite,
While jellyfish float, a translucent sight.

Breezes carry laughter across the bay,
As fireflies dance and night leads the way.
Each grain of sand holds a giggle or two,
In this vibrant realm where dreams come true.

Elysium of Hidden Lagoons

Lush palms wave like they're in a dance,
In hidden nooks, there's a splashy romance.
A frog croaks jokes on a lily pad throne,
While dragonflies laugh at a sneaky stone.

The water's winks sparkle and tease,
As fish tell tales with each gentle breeze.
Crickets drum on a moonlit night,
While owls hoot, sharing their flight.

Coconuts drop with a comedic thud,
As turtles join in for a splashy mud.
Frothy waves giggle as they roll,
Each rippling echo a happy soul.

Mystical lands with secrets to keep,
Where laughter glimmers and dreams leap.
In this whimsical world, all hearts align,
As nature plays tricks, oh what a design!

Sentinels of Time in Coral Reefs

Coral towers stand with a goofy grin,
Fish swim by in a colorful spin.
Anemones tickle all passing fins,
As laughter bubbles where life begins.

Sea urchins wear their spikes with pride,
While shells host parties that swell with tide.
A clownfish jokes with a Anemone's sway,
In this ocean circus, we laugh and play.

Octopuses juggle with eight wiggly arms,
Chasing away dullness with their charms.
Seas cucumbers squirm in silly delight,
Making waves of giggles throughout the night.

Time flies here like a fluttering breeze,
In this watery land, we do as we please.
With colorful whispers, the sea tells tales,
Of quirks and laughter where wonder prevails.

Tales Carried by the Moonlight

In the dark, two crabs argue,
One claims he saw a star,
The other laughs, says that can't be true,
It's just a glow from the bar.

They dance on sand, like silly fools,
As the tide rolls in and out,
Spinning tales of jellyfish schools,
With laughter, filling the air with clout.

A clam plays drums on a seaweed beat,
While fish join in with glee,
The moon winks down, tapping its feet,
As the ocean hums a melody.

So if you roam where the tides embrace,
Look for crabs with a tale or two,
Under moonlight, they find their place,
In this world where dreams come true.

Fluctuations in the Silken Surf

The waves all wiggle in a prankster's show,
Slapping fish with a giggle, oh no!
Seagulls squawk, trying to take a shot,
While the tide hides treasures, forgot or not.

A starfish tries to do a ballet spin,
But stumbles right into a clam's chin,
With a 'sorry' and a chuckle, they both flop,
While the seaweed sways, they just can't stop.

A dolphin zooms by, playing hide and seek,
With a splash and a burst of laughter, so sleek,
As shells bounce around, joining the game,
The surf's a merry mess; who's to blame?

When the sun sets low, painting skies bright,
The beach becomes a stage, pure delight,
In this party of nature, fun is swift,
Every wave has a story, a jolly gift.

Resonance of Hidden Lagoons

In a hidden cove where secrets bloom,
A tortoise sings to a loud vacuum,
The echo resounds, making all jump high,
While frogs croak along, oh my, oh my!

An otter slides down a mossy slope,
With a splash he creates, a slippery rope,
The fish giggle, swimming in place,
While the sun peeks in with a cheeky face.

Lagoons are filled with tales of the weird,
Where octopus paint like a wizard cheered,
They swirl and twirl, colors all free,
Creating portraits of their jubilee.

As night sneaks in and stars start to wink,
Creatures gather close on the edge of the brink,
With laughter and joy, their hearts unite,
In this place of magic, under starlit night.

The Enchanted Cove's Breath

The cove takes a breath, a giggly sigh,
A crab flips backflips, oh me, oh my!
Sea turtles chuckle, in slow-motion grace,
While a flounder plays cards, keeping pace.

Anemones wave like they're in a dance,
Fish dressed in stripes take a wild chance,
As bubbles float up, filled with laughter,
Who knew the sea could be such a crafter?

The moon dips low, whispering jokes,
To the clam with pearls, surrounded by folks,
Seagulls cackle, the sun bows low,
As the cove breathes life, ready to glow.

With echoes of joy on the salty wave,
Creatures unite, their spirits brave,
In this enchanted place, fun never fades,
In the heartbeat of laughter, memory cascades.

Rhythm of the Coral Dreams

Beneath the waves, the fish do dance,
In bubble hats, they take a chance.
With every swish, a giggle loud,
Crustaceans join, they're feeling proud.

Octopus plays the drums with style,
While sea turtles swim the extra mile.
A jellyfish winks, oh what a sight,
In the coral dreams, it's pure delight.

Seahorses wear their finest threads,
In a majestic ballet, they tread.
A dolphin sings, the notes go wild,
Under the sea, every creature's a child.

With frothy laughter and playful glee,
The ocean's pulse is wild and free.
A conch shell voice gives a booming cheer,
In the rhythm of dreams, there's nothing to fear.

Pulse of the Wind-Whipped Waves

The breeze tickles, like a friendly tease,
Seagulls squawk, doing as they please.
Waves crash high, they splatter and spin,
In the surf's wild dance, we all dive in.

Surfboards wobble, folks take a fall,
The ocean laughs, a grand old haul.
Flip-flops flying, it's chaos galore,
As laughter rings from the sandy shore.

Youngsters build castles, grand and tall,
Only to watch the waves claim them all.
But even though, they'll start anew,
With buckets and spades, that's what they do.

In wind-whipped waves, the fun's a blast,
With silly stories from the past.
The ocean's pulse runs strong and bright,
A splash of joy in the golden light.

Secrets Beneath Sapphire Skies

Up above, the seabirds swoop and dive,
While below, the clownfish come alive.
With googly eyes and a playful wink,
They plot a prank more than you think.

The ocean floor hides secret treasures,
Like old lost shoes and surfer's pleasures.
A treasure map? It's just a joke,
A sea turtle chuckles, and gives a poke.

Pearl oysters gossip, oh what a sight,
Filling tidbits with great delight.
Crabs play charades, they pinch and prance,
Even a starfish knows how to dance.

In sapphire skies, the secrets swirl,
Underneath, a comical whirl.
The ocean's tales, a giggle or two,
With each wave's story, it starts anew.

Serenade of the Lagoon

In the lagoon, the frogs sing loud,
A raucous choir, they're feeling proud.
With croaks and ribbits, they set the stage,
In the moonlit night, they earn the wage.

Bubbles rise as the fish join in,
A splashy tango, let the fun begin!
Flamingos sway with legs so long,
In this wild concert, it's all a song.

Fireflies blink like disco lights,
While the shrimp do the twist, oh what sights!
Amidst the reeds, laughter flows,
The lagoon's magic only grows.

As night falls soft, the music plays,
With giggling creatures, the lagoon sways.
A serenade of joy and cheer,
In this vibrant world, we shed a tear.

Harmonics of the Salt-Kissed Breeze

In the sun, the seagulls tease,
Dancing on the salty breeze.
They squawk about the juicy feast,
Fish tacos made by a quirky beast.

Waves roll in with sandy flair,
Shells become the stages there.
Crabs clap claws in rhythmic cheer,
While flopping fish make jokes we hear.

The palm trees sway with playful groans,
Whispering secrets in funny tones.
In this place where laughter grows,
Nature's humor often shows.

From the shore to the ocean's edge,
There's comedy that won't allege.
Each splash and giggle quite absurd,
In the rhythm of the sea, we're stirred.

Serenade of the Misty Tropics

In the morning, misty and light,
Monkeys swing with sheer delight.
They steal bananas, don't you see?
Making a ruckus in the treetops free.

Coconuts drop with a thud and roll,
Sipping from them is quite the goal.
But watch your head, and take great care,
For pesky parrots might just stare!

Sunsets bring the critters out,
Lively chats, there's never doubt.
Frogs in tuxedos sing a tune,
To the fireflies' bright, glowing boon.

Tropical charm with laughs galore,
Every hour we crave for more.
Humor thrives in leafy lanes,
In this paradise, joy reigns!

Melodies from the Lush Canopy

In the trees, the monkeys play,
Swinging in a goofy way.
With every leap, a silly sound,
Echoes through the green playground.

Parrots chat in colors bright,
Trading gossip, what a sight!
They cackle, honk, and squawk away,
As if to say, it's their whole day.

Lizards lounge with lazy flair,
Posing like they just don't care.
Bugs perform a tiny dance,
While flowers laugh at the sun's glance.

In the jungle, laughter blooms,
With all its quirky little rooms.
In this world, so lush and wide,
The melodies of fun abide.

The Tide's Secret Lullaby

As the tide rolls back and forth,
Shells whisper tales of mirth.
Turtles giggle with slow grace,
As they navigate the watery space.

The ocean sighs, a friendly tease,
Tickling toes in the gentle breeze.
Jellyfish float with a squishy grin,
In this playground, nobody's thin.

Sandcastles bloom but quickly fall,
The waves come crashing, having a ball.
Kids run back, arms flailing high,
Chasing seafoam as it whizzes by.

At dusk, the stars begin to gleam,
Night brings laughter, a glowing dream.
With each wave, a story spins,
In the rhythm, joy always wins.

Voyage of the Restless Souls

On a boat made of dreams and squeaky toys,
We drift through the fog, just a bunch of boys.
With seagulls that laugh and fish that tease,
Our treasure map's written in a long, lost breeze.

Every wave is a giggle, each splash a cheer,
We dance with the sea, no worries nor fear.
A pirate's life, full of jellyfish pranks,
We toast with sea foam, and give fish high ranks.

The stars in the sky wear silly hats,
While turtles join in, with their dance and chats.
With a compass that spins, we twirl in delight,
Adventurous fluffballs, oh what a sight!

So here's to the journey, the silly and strange,
With laughter and mischief, we'll always exchange.
In this wavy serenade where whimsy lays,
We ride on giggles for the rest of our days.

Swaying to Nature's Melody

The palm trees sway like they're on a spree,
Singing to crabs that dance by the sea.
Oh, the coconut choir, so off-key yet sweet,
Even the squirrels have tapped their feet.

The sun's a big comedian, roasting our skin,
While our flip-flops play tag, let the fun begin!
A splash here, a squawk there, it's chaos divine,
Nature's own circus, all tangled in vine.

The breeze tells jokes that float through the air,
As fish wink at us, without a single care.
With seashells as trumpets, and waves as our band,
In this rhythm of laughter, we perfectly stand.

So let's sway together, in this playful dance,
Where nature sings loud, and we all take a chance.
With sandcastles crumbling, but spirits so high,
We'll party with seaweed beneath the bright sky.

Beneath the Canopy of Dreams

In a treehouse made of giggles and cheers,
We hide from the world, with no pesky peers.
The branches are tickling our curious minds,
Beneath a sky where wonder unwinds.

Squirrels play tag, the owls hoot a tune,
While moonbeams dance, lightheartedly swoon.
A hammock of laughter swings to and fro,
In a whimsical world, where we steal the show.

The leaves whisper secrets, oh so absurd,
While frogs croon ballads, all utterly heard.
In this leafy retreat, we dream without pause,
Inventing our stories, with playful applause.

With stars as our audience, we put on a play,
As fireflies flash, and we dance the night away.
In this canopy woven with giggles and schemes,
Life's nothing but laughter, beneath our bold dreams.

Breathe of the Cerulean Sea

A bubble of laughter floats over the waves,
As fish wear top hats and become our braves.
Crabs juggle seashells, the clams sing a song,
In this watery world, we all dance along.

The surf's a comedian, making us laugh,
While starfish play poker, a curious craft.
With dolphins that prank us, diving with zest,
We're guests in their party, oh what a jest!

The breeze brings us tales, all salty and sweet,
With seagulls stealing fries, oh what a treat.
As tides roll in laughter, we shout with glee,
Each splash adds a punchline to our jubilee.

So come join the fun, in spirits so free,
Where the sea tells jokes, and we catch glee.
With waves that giggle and skies that gleam,
We breathe in the magic, and ride on a dream.

A Harmonious Song of Solitude

In a hammock so wide, I sway and I grin,
A coconut falls, and I dodge with a spin.
The crab in the sand is my dance partner, tight,
We two-step through shadows till the end of the night.

Seagulls above sing tunes quite absurd,
Each squawk is a note, oh haven't you heard?
With a wink and a nod, they steal all my fries,
I laugh as they dive, not a care in the skies.

A fish flicks its tail, flips my thoughts to the sea,
It wiggles and jigs, what a sight to see!
But oh, when it's lunchtime, it's eyes on my plate,
I sigh yet again, it's just hard to keep straight.

So here in my haven of sun and of play,
I dance to the rhythm of a carefree day.
With laughter like bubbles, the moments float by,
This solo delight, oh so sweet, oh so sly!

Ebb and Flow of Ancient Echoes

The waves give a chuckle, they tease and they taunt,
Telling tales of mermaids who giggle and flaunt.
With seaweed as hats, they twirl through the brine,
While I squint and ponder, 'Are those creatures fine?'

A crab fits in snug with my flip-flop shoe,
It pinches my toe; it's a friendly debut.
While dolphins jump high, they flip with a cheer,
Inviting me over, while I sip my beer.

Whispers in shells echo stories so old,
Of pirate's lost treasures and adventures bold.
Yet here on the shore, not a worry in sight,
Just laughter and mischief till the fall of night.

So bring on the tides, let them do their best,
With a wink and a smile, I'm just here for the jest.
For even the ocean has moments to jest,
A comedy show where I'm lucky, I guess!

Chants of Seagulls at Dusk

Seagulls in suits, what a sight on the breeze,
They argue and squawk, as if planning a tease.
One grabs a fish taco, spills salsa and guac,
While I laugh at the messy little flock.

As dusk settles low, they gather and squabble,
Like kids in a playground, they squeak and they hobble.
A long-winded story gets lost in their bite,
With feathers in disarray, oh what a delight.

Their shouts fill the air like an off-key song,
With a chorus of chaos, where do I belong?
Yet I laugh at their antics, such silly old birds,
Creating a banquet of jokes without words.

With shadows now dancing and colors ablaze,
I join in the chaos, lost in the haze.
For here with the gulls, I could dance 'til I'm sore,
Life's a funny charade, and I'm always wanting more!

The Rhythm of Coral Reefs

Beneath the blue water, where fish prance and twirl,
A clown fish is joking; oh what a wild swirl!
With colors that pop, they put on a spree,
A party of scales just dancing with glee.

An octopus winks from the corner with style,
Changing its colors like it's swayed the aisle.
While turtles glide by with a leisurely scoff,
Dog-paddling skeptics, never too far off.

Bubble-blowing fish create laughter so bright,
Their bloops fill the ocean, like bubbles of light.
With corals that shimmy, they join in the play,
Every splash tells a story beneath the enfant, sway.

So here's to the reefs with their wonders so true,
Each creature a comedian, every hue a view.
In this underwater realm, joy runs deep and wide,
With laughter and mirth, the ocean's playful guide!

Chants from the Ocean's Depths

Bubbles rise like party cheers,
Tickling fish with silly fears.
Octopus does the cha-cha slide,
While crabs on dance floors take their pride.

Jellyfish jive with glowing flair,
Seahorses giggle, without a care.
Clams are gossiping, oh so sly,
Underwater antics make me sigh.

Turtles race in slow-motion glee,
Hydrodynamic arguments like a spree.
Sharks disguise in funny hats,
Making friends with curious spats.

Eels electrify the party sound,
While starfish spin around and around.
Anemones puff with pride and strut,
Where humor swims, the world is a nut.

Fables of the Lapping Water

Waves tell tales of sunken shoes,
Mermaid's laughter, colorful hues.
Fishes gossip about the moon,
While waves dance like fans to a tune.

Flapping gulls create the buzz,
Seashells whisper, "Oh, what a fuss!"
Crabs tell stories of night's parade,
With sailors lost in an orange shade.

Barnacles hold onto old lore,
Listening closely to the ocean's score.
Pelicans dive into the fray,
While dolphins play tag, oh what a day!

Shells meet for a fancy feast,
Where sea cucumbers are the least.
Giggling waves together sail,
Creating laughter inside each tale.

Heartbeats in the Shipping Lanes

Boats honk like geese on a spree,
Cargo clinks with laughter, oh me!
Sailors swap stories of wild tide,
As GPS winks with even more pride.

Lighthouses waltz in their glow,
Guiding tired ships to and fro.
Whales join in with big belly flops,
Sending waves up to the sky that pops.

Fish catch wind of the shipping lanes,
Laughing away their salty gains.
Anchor chains rattle like pots and pans,
As gulls drop in with their odd, funny plans.

The harbor's alive with tales and cheers,
Echoing dreams from sailors' years.
With every ripple and wave that plays,
The funny heart of the sea relays.

Harmony of the Fisherman's Tale

Fishers hum as their nets they cast,
With hopes of dinner, they sing quite fast.
The catch of the day is full of tricks,
Dancing in buckets, making picks.

Hooks are tangled in stories spun,
"Caught a big one!"—despite no fun.
Campsite laughter from the shore aches,
As fishing lines weave maidens' fakes.

Seaspray jokes mix with evening stew,
While crabs parade in worn-out shoes.
The moon winks at the comedy play,
As fish wish for freedom, but stay at bay.

With every cast and every laugh,
The ocean swirls in a lively draught.
Harmony floats on waves, oh what joy,
Fishing's a game for every girl and boy.

Silhouettes in the Glow of Dusk

In the shadows we dance with glee,
Spinning tales of coconut tea.
A crab scuttles by, thinks it's so sly,
While seagulls above just laugh and fly.

The sunset winks at a banana boat,
As we waddle and trip wearing a float.
Mangoes tumble from trees so ripe,
We giggle till we roll, what a ripe type!

With flip-flops squeaking on sandy track,
We chase our dreams, then lose our snacks.
An octopus waves, cool as can be,
While we fumble like kids, oh what a spree!

As day bows out, the stars appear,
We toast with coconuts and share a cheer.
In this glowing dusk where mirth ignites,
Laughter echoes into the starry nights.

Wanderlust of the Untrodden Paths

We put on hats, yes four or five,
Exploring paths that never thrive.
A chicken squawks, tells us to go,
But we're lost in the vibes, as you might know.

The compass spins like a child on a spree,
Leading us to a party, not a sea.
With wristbands from last year's fête,
We dance in circles—it's never too late!

Tiki torches flicker, and we trip, trip, trip,
Over each other, we laugh and flip.
A map in our hands, but where's the fun?
As a tourist we wander, we've just begun!

'Untrodden' paths full of splashes and giggles,
Like finding a treasure full of tickles.
Come join us here, you might just find,
That lost is the best way to unwind!

Heartbeats in the Coral Garden

In a garden where the fishes play,
We wear goggles and splash like it's ballet.
Coral blooms, in colors so bright,
It's a fashion show, underwater delight!

Anemones wave, what a lovely sight,
As we flail around, quite a fright!
A turtle rolls by with a cheeky grin,
We shout, 'Hey buddy, let's swim again!'

With bubbles rising like our goofy laughs,
We tickle the seaweed, take crazy paths.
Each heart that beats in this azure land,
Is dancing with joy, together we stand.

With seashells gathered and laughter galore,
We'll sing with the dolphins till our voices are sore.
In this coral garden, we've truly found,
Laughter and joy in the ocean's sound.

Secrets of the Midnight Isle

At midnight we gather, whispers abound,
With flashlights on our faces, we make silly sounds.
The moon's our chef, cooking dreams in the dark,
As we stumble on sand and chase after a shark!

A palm tree wobbling, bends low for a snack,
Curious crabs think we're a friendly pack.
We tell ghost stories, with twists oh so wild,
'Were those really shadows or just sea's wild child?'

Twinkling stars eavesdrop on our cheeky quests,
While fireflies compete in their brightest vests.
We moonwalk the beach, giggling in fright,
As owls hold their laughter; oh, what a sight!

In the heart of the night, our voices combine,
To tell all the secrets of rocking divine.
With every chuckle and every bright smile,
Midnight's our canvas, on this wild isle!

Beneath the Sky's Embrace

A crab dances sideways, quick and spry,
Doing the cha-cha while seagulls fly.
The sun wears shades, sipping on a drink,
While fish join the whirlpool, don't you think?

A coconut laughs, rolling down the sand,
Waves tickle toes from the ocean's hand.
Flip-flops are chirping, what a funny sight,
As the tide winks back, full of delight.

Jellyfish bounce like soft marshmallows,
In a flamboyant dance, looking quite shallow.
The beach ball giggles as it takes a dive,
Splashing sea turtles, who can't quite thrive.

Even the sunsets wear colorful hues,
As crabs crack jokes in loud oceanic crews.
Laughter is carried on salt-scented air,
Beneath the sky's embrace, all woes we share.

Stars Reflected in Ocean's Pulse

Stars twinkle like beads on the ocean's dress,
While fish flip around, in sequined finesse.
One shark wears a tie for a midnight feast,
With a wink and a sigh, 'I'm the underwater beast!'

Moonbeams play hopscotch, soft on the waves,
Octopuses rave like they're dancing slaves.
A whale takes a selfie, with dolphins in tow,
'Look at my fins!' they cheer, putting on a show.

The tide plays the drums, in a rhythmic flow,
As clams shout, 'Encore!', putting on a glow.
Mermaids gossip, knitting nets of gold,
While starfish attempt to tell tales of old.

Midnight snacks all around—seaweed and cheese,
The ocean's a party, put your mind at ease.
In this watery ballroom, where echoes collide,
Stars reflected laugh, as they take us for a ride.

Whispers of the Tide

The waves giggle softly as they tease the shore,
While crabs pull pranks, begging for more.
Seashells gossip under sandy blankets,
About starfish who strut, 'Aren't we so splendid?'

The tide whispers secrets in a frothy rush,
As flip-flops clamor, creating a fuss.
Pelicans dive in like they're on a spree,
Nabbing lunch while we're sipping iced tea.

Seagulls squawk riddles—what's brown and white?
A confused pelican, lost in mid-flight.
The ocean chuckles, rocking its cradle,
As barnacles dance on a floating fable.

Between the salty giggles, laughter sways,
What's the fish's favorite game? 'Catch the rays!'
With waves as our chorus, and sand as our floor,
Let's dance to the whispers, forever and more.

Echoes of Ancient Shores

Old stones remember the tales of the deep,
As the sea creeps in, starting to leap.
Laughter of past sailors rides on the breeze,
With each wave that crashes, they're still at ease.

Fish throw a banquet, their seaweed delight,
While dolphins compete with their high-flying flight.
Seashells take bets on the fastest fin,
As mermaids cheer, their fiesta to win.

Sand dollars chime in with a friendly clink,
About pirates who once made a ship's sink.
Elders of the sea laugh with pure delight,
As the sun waves 'bye' and gives way to night.

Echoes of stories swirl up in the air,
Each tide brings a chuckle, a twist to share.
The shores are alive with capers galore,
With ancient echoes that always implore.

Fabric of the Seafoam

In the depths of frothy dreams,
Seaweed dances, or so it seems.
Tiny fish throw a wildcard,
Making waves like a bard.

Crabs wear hats, a fashion show,
Snails glide by, with grace and slow.
Ocean's pulse beats with a grin,
Who knew the fish could wear a fin?

Seashells chatter on the shore,
Sharing gossip, tales of yore.
Jellyfish float in jeweled coats,
While plankton twirl, and the sea gloat.

Laughter echoes through the tide,
As seagulls giggle, side by side.
Life beneath a frothy shimmy,
Turns out ocean's quite the filmy!

Twilight Murmurs of Forgotten Lore

As sun dips low, the stars arrive,
Whispers of mermaids start to thrive.
Fish trade secrets in drunken glee,
Octopus offers ink for free!

The lighthouse blinks like it's in on the joke,
A wise old turtle, he's no mere yolk.
With every splash, a story swells,
About a clam that rings doorbells!

Waves chuckle softly, tickling the sand,
The night pulls a prank, can you understand?
Stars wink down, glinting like cash,
As crabs hold a dance, in a light-hearted bash.

Burbling voices fill the sea,
As dolphins break out, wild and free.
In this twilight, laughter raves,
The ocean's secrets, nobody saves!

Aeons of Spirits in Calm Waters

In stillness lies a ghostly tale,
Of merry fish who paddle and flail.
With flip-flops on, they strut about,
Claiming they're the sea's best scout!

Whales hum tunes from ages past,
Kraken joins in with a thundering blast.
Eons pass in a playful cheer,
As the tide rolls on with nothing to fear.

Old seaweed tells jokes, oh so punny,
While barnacles laugh, feeling quite funny.
Every splash has a story to break,
In amusing waves, they silently quake.

Bubbles rise, they float so high,
Little creatures wave goodbye.
As the moon pulls laughter from below,
We sail on dreams, in this watery show!

Ephemeral Caresses of the Surf

Waves roll in with a playful tease,
Kissing the shore with salty ease.
Sandy toes, a sandy grin,
The surf whispers secrets and sin.

Seagulls squawk a silly tune,
While clams hold their breath by the moon.
Tides tickle feet, making us shriek,
As sandcastles giggle, unique and sleek.

A sea breeze dances, flailing hair,
Shells clink together, giggling fair.
With every splash, joy holds its sway,
In this fun pool of sunlit play!

So here we are, the beach so bright,
Surf's sweet laughter, a pure delight.
As day draws close and stars take flight,
The ocean winks, "Come back tomorrow night!"

Vibrations of Forgotten Tales

In shadows where the coconuts sway,
A crab tells tales of the bright sun's play.
With flip-flops dancing near the shore,
Seagulls squawk, 'Oh, give us more!'

Old fishermen tell jokes to the fish,
Who swim and wish for a sun-kissed dish.
'Why did the octopus cross the sea?'
To find a shell with a cup of tea!

The waves giggle as they roll and crash,
Tickling toes in an oceanic splash.
Starfish laugh under the moonlit night,
While crabs recite sonnets of delight.

And when the tide begins to rise,
The seashells hum their ballads, oh so wise.
With each wave's beat, the stories grow,
As laughter echoes, a playful flow.

Threads of Nature's Whisper

A gecko struts on a branch with flair,
Reciting rhymes without a care.
Lizards sing to the buzzing bees,
While coconut trees dance in the breeze.

Anemones wave like they've found a tune,
While sea turtles moonwalk by the dune.
The sand whispers secrets oh-so-soft,
As crabs don tiny hats and scoff.

The sun winks at the passing waves,
As laughter drifts from the coral caves.
With every twist of the tidal dance,
Even the rocks seem to prance!

In this realm where silliness grows,
Nature's threads weave where humor flows.
Here, every critter knows how to play,
In this land where joy leads the way.

Glimmers in the Midnight Tide

At midnight, the sea's a comedy show,
With dolphins acting like they don't know.
The moon giggles as it splashes bright,
While starfish throw a disco delight.

Crabs put on makeup and strut their stuff,
Saying, 'Honey, we are more than tough!'
The jellyfish swing like they own the scene,
In the twinkling waters, all glowing and green.

An octopus juggles shells with a grin,
As the seaweed sways, cheering, 'Let's begin!'
Every wave that crashes feels just like a jest,
As laughter from the tide becomes a quest.

So here in the dark where the waters giggle,
Life's more fun with every little wiggle.
Join the dance and feel the flow,
As the midnight tide puts on a show!

Flows of the Ocean's Pulse

The ocean's pulse beats with a quirk,
Where fish throw parties and seahorses lurk.
Each wave's a giggle, a bubble of jest,
With oysters creating their best treasure chest.

The shells chime softly like bells of glass,
While clams tap-dance on seaweed grass.
A pelican jokes as it dives for a snack,
And the barnacles cheer, 'Don't hold back!'

Starry skies dump whims into the sea,
While playful sea otters dance with glee.
Shark dons a tutu, what a sight to see,
While turtles chuckle, 'Oh, let us be free!'

So come join the fun in these waters vast,
Where nature's humor flutters and casts.
With each tiny ripple, laughter grows bright,
As the ocean pulses with pure delight.

www.ingramcontent.com/pod-product-compliance
Lightning Source LLC
Chambersburg PA
CBHW052221090526
44585CB00015BA/1425